The Grace of Ordinary Days

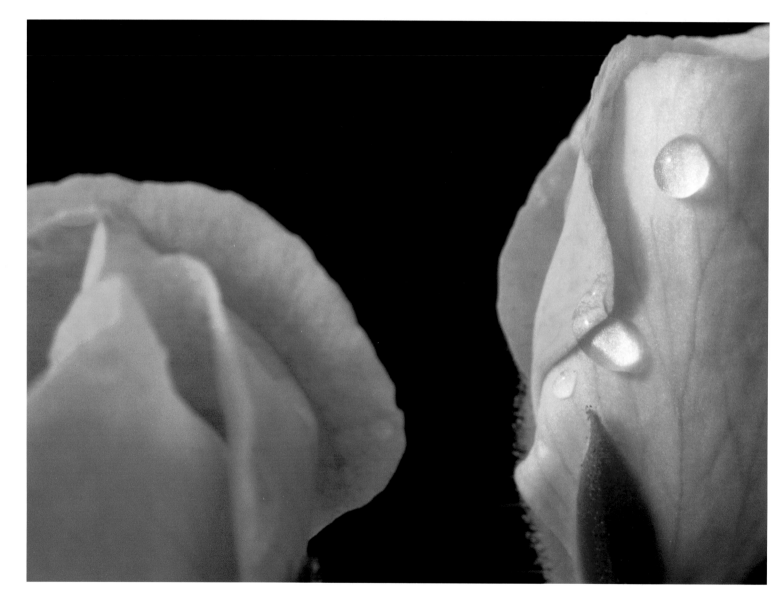

AN INVITATION
TO CELEBRATE
LIFE'S JOURNEY

The Grace of Ordinary Days

Kay Saunders &
Bernie Saunders

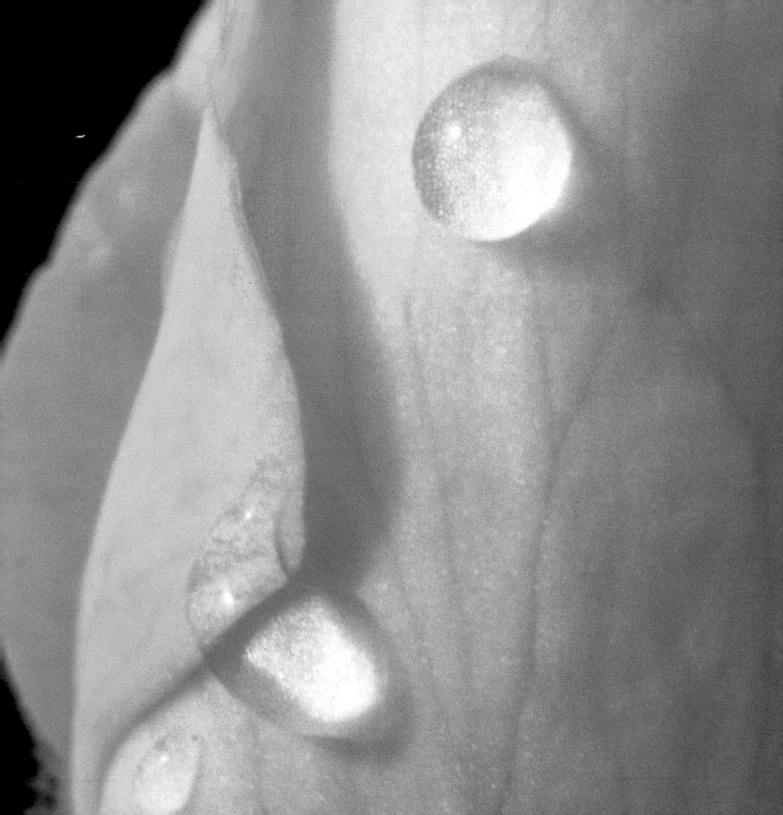

Dedication

To my parents, Kay and George Saunders,

loving co-creators who helped

breathe life into this book.

Contents

Contents

Foreword

There is an appointed time for everything. A time to be born, and a time to die. A time to plant, and a time to uproot the plant. A time to weep, and a time to laugh. A time to mourn and a time to dance. A time to be silent and a time to speak. I was reminded of this passage from Ecclesiastes the moment I opened *The Grace of Ordinary Days*. Both are a life-affirming reminder of nature's seasons as well as the four stages of human life: birth, youth, maturity, and death. I was drawn in by the book's immediate beauty and the intricate weaving of life stories and art and poetry. This is a reflective book about the ordinary and extraordinary seasons of life, a collaboration between a mother and son. It is the story of a woman who made peace with a lifelong illness and found countless ways of transforming her life experience into poetry, offering everything her mind and body could possibly give. It is the story of a man who discovered the art of nature photography and his surprise at the unexpected creative force that led him to a new way of embracing the world and his mother. What they offered one another was a sense of tenderness, a way of embracing both the light and dark sweep of memory. And what they offer you, the reader, is a way of embarking on your own journey of self-discovery.

The poet, Anaïs Nin, said, *And the day came when the pain of remaining tight in a bud was greater than the risk it took to open.* When Kay and Bernie Saunders made the commitment of creating *The Grace of Ordinary Days* they became kindred souls, a friendship that expanded far beyond their mother and son relationship. They learned that the deepest stories are those we give one another, that the very act of telling and listening, giving and receiving can form a bridge from one heart to another.

Perhaps *The Grace of Ordinary Days* will serve as a mirror for you and will inspire you to lean into the rich experiences of life that move through all of us. What are the stories you tell and retell? The stories we must attend to in order to communicate with those we love? The stories that must come alive in order to find ourselves in one another?

There is a strong need for this book. A book about mothers and sons is rare and has been a long time coming. I am grateful for *The Grace of Ordinary Days*. I invite you to enter the photographs and breathe in their beauty, to let the poems and reflections come alive, to speak to a deeper wisdom, to the unspoken stories of your life. If there is a relationship in your life that needs expanding, enriching, or mending, this book can be an extraordinary gift, a new language, a new way of communicating, an offering of love and healing.

ELLEN KORT

Poet Laureate of Wisconsin

2000 - 2004

The Invitation

It is true that women of the world give birth, and it is a mighty thing. My mother used to say that birthing was the easy part, having birthed and raised five children. There will be forever that linkage, that translucent thread of years that holds us together. I went through all the varied seasons of outgrowing my childhood, sometimes stretching beyond the limits my mother tried to set for me. I was not always sure I could meet her expectations. She was a tenacious teacher, wanting the best for me. We survived those years, and when I married and had children of my own I realized just how much she taught me about the human circle of love.

Both my mother and I found our artistic endeavors during our fifties. I became a professional photographer and my mother a published poet. What we found was that each of us had discovered a way of exploring the world from a wise and creative place. We had navigated our way through the years and found not only acceptance, but also a new understanding as artistic peers ~ a radiance spun from the blood-strong closeness of a parent and child. The one thing we most wanted to do was to collaborate on a book, my close-up photos of flowers and her poetry.

This was not easy, as Mom was frail and in ill health. She struggled to put the "just-right" words on paper. She died before this book was completed and it was up to me to become a birth-giver. I remembered her words, "birthing is the easy part," and thought how can that be? I wanted to honor her, to give life to the book and her poems. My father and I had long conversations about it and I welcomed his growing involvement and resolve. We realized that the book was as much about the relationship between mother and son as it was about flowers and poetry ~ a narrative in two voices. After my mother's death, her friend and poet, Patricia Reckrey, served as her spirit writer to finish the stories with me. In the wake of my mother's transition to her new life I see that this book has taken on a life of its own. It has created an invitation for anyone who reads it to rediscover what is already his or hers.

The Grace of Ordinary Days is now in your hands. My mother and I have sung its song, breathed it into being. Someone once said our lives depend on the stories we tell. Perhaps you will find a part of your own story here and we invite you to contemplate the special moments of your life and be moved to share them with a parent, child, a sibling, or other loved ones.

Bernie Saunders – *May, 2005*

CONCEPTION

I thought it was just a pleasant summer visit until Bernie proposed a book project. His photographs. My poems. A book celebrating a mother's and son's life journey - our journey - and in telling our story, an invitation to others to explore the ins and outs of their lives. Interested? he asked. There are no words for my enthusiasm and excitement about it.

And there are no words for my fears. I know this 80-year-old body of mine is frail beyond imagining. A lifetime of asthma and now this persistent back pain and the

intestinal bouts have left me ravaged. My spirit is willing, but this flesh? Will I be able to hold up my end of the project? Will I ever see it completed?

I want to begin. Right now.

There's a Swedish proverb:
Those who wish to sing always
find a song.

We want to sing.
We'll find a song....

— KAY

She went for it big time. Her poems.
My photographs. A book celebrating our life.
An invitation to others to honor their journey.

The kernel of an idea has sprouted into a big deal. It's grown to be the focal point of our 60 years together. Rebellion, love, guilt, understanding, and forgiveness. Normal garden-variety neurotic stuff between a mother and son. She says, "We better hurry."

Why would I want to do a book with my mother when our relationship has not always been in concert with each other? Because she's my mother, the only mother I have, and I love her.

— BERNIE

~ EARLY YEARS ~

THE RAVINE

I was an only child born when my parents were older. I spent a lot of time dreaming of imaginary brothers and sisters who would play board games or dolls with me. I decided early that when I married we would have a house full of kids who would spend time together and enjoy one another. That idealized picture was way too tame for this brood of five brothers and sisters.

On summer days like today this place is alive with the comings and goings of my five children and a crew of neighbor kids. Our house is their stop-through spot on the way to the ravine.

All the action is down there. The house is where they come for a sandwich when they're hungry, for a Band-Aid when a knee is torn open, or to engage me as a referee when a fight can't be settled any other way.

I often think of Virginia Wolfe's quote of a woman needing a room of her own. But I know kids must need their own "rooms" too, and the ravine has become their place. I'm happy for them but I must admit when I watch them playing so happily down there, I feel again the loneliness of being an "only."

— KAY

Oh boy, freedom! I just erased my last chore off the board in the back hallway, so now Mom says I can go to the ravine. It rained last night and I can't wait to find out if the creek overflowed.

Wow, look at how fast the water is going! It's perfect for building dams and for stick boat races.

The house may be Mom's castle, but the ravine is mine. Endless bike trails, secret hideouts, bullfrogs, flying squirrels, snapping turtles, and a huge tree fort. And Mom doesn't mind if I'm covered in mud.

(What does the ravine smell like? Colors? Sounds? What does it feel like when you're inside the tree fort?)

Mom calls us from the end of the peninsula of our yard, "Time to come in for dinner, kids."

I hope we can have a campfire tonight, and stay up late to fill a Mason jar with fireflies.

— BERNIE

Come with Me

down under

only ten steps

into yesterday

Only a glimpse

of my youth

in the cracked mirror

Run your hand

over rusty ice skates

Grandpa's shotgun

snowshoes bowling balls

Take note of

travel journals

Italy Ireland Canada

Corsica Moldy maps

might show you the way

Refill empty shoe boxes

vases baskets

Mason jars

Imagine the drone

of the treadle sewing machine

its drawers full of

bobbins buttons

bias tape lace

Come with me

into yesterday

In the Parlor

Framed in ornate gold,

Little Lord Fauntleroy

in velvet suit and buckled shoes

looks on as guests sit

on our green velour settee

and on the window seat which holds

a Sears Roebuck catalogue

McCalls, Saturday Evening Post

and the phone book.

Mother winds the Victrola

that polished prize

with shiny, gold handle.

It grumbles and growls

finally a Sousa march

or "Oh, Suzannah"—

"Oh, Suzannah" spinning on our Victrola,

me spinning around the room.

Mother thought I was

the only entertainment for company.

Get that Damn Elephant
Off My Chest

When I was five

an elephant sat on my chest

and wouldn't move.

He found me lying in a field

of timothy, whistling, with a blade

between my lips,

watching sheep dance in the sky.

Every year he grew

heavier and uglier

the doctors and nurses

tried to chase him away

with needles and pills

to make me gasp

to make me exhausted

to make pain wedge itself

into deeper wrinkles.

When I was five

an elephant sat on my chest

and hasn't left.

From an Only Child

Maybe they said let's try again

this time it might go

to fruition.

Maybe they said as they cuddled,

huddled in flannel nightgowns,

listening to the snowplow rumble

the furnace grumble

and she said yes

the wind wails

around the corner of this bedroom.

He said we are here,

we are warm,

nothing can hurt us,

nothing can deter us

from trying again

from hoping this act of love

this dream

out of season

will be a Christmas present

to be unwrapped in August.

Reflection   jar of dandelions

clutched in his sweaty fist

precious gift for Mom

Has Anyone Seen the Little Girl Who Used to Live Here?

the one with wavy brown hair

smiling eyes

that cried too easily

too often

the little girl who carried a rosary in one pocket

black licorice and a hankie in the other

who wore a gold locket

on her white blouse

the same one stitched with pink French knots?

Has anyone seen the little girl

who giggled at the smallest joke

who needed more hugs than scoldings

the same one who rocked her twin baby dolls

while she sat on the porch swing

watching the maple leaves turn and tremble

before the rain?

Has anyone heard of her?

I'm looking for someone who knew her

someone who remembers

and will tell me

if she's ever written a poem

loved a man

cuddled a baby?

Fireflies and Prayers

A full moon throws a beam

across your bed

exposes tan, hard legs

tough from football and soccer.

Startled

I step back,

wonder where

the little boy went.

Wasn't it last night

I tiptoed in to say

prayers with you

evening prayers and hugs,

fireflies blinking

between blades of grass?

Conflict

No, I wasn't ready for his adolescence

But there it was standing in the door

Tall, lean and defiant:

I sat rocking, my dress still rumpled

from his baby hugs;

shoes run down from chasing after him;

Eyes still shiny with love of his innocence;

Arms crooked, aching to hold and protect him,

But there he stood, my son,

Tall, lean and defiant.

Reflection speak to me of life

straight sturdy stem

love's promise

WAITING UP

It's late. Too late. Where is he?

It was so much easier when I knew he was tucked in upstairs sleeping as soundly as the other four. Who was it that said we must give our children a warm nest and strong wings? The nest's the easy part, but, ah, to give them wings!

I know he's begun drinking. I talk to him about it, but he can't hear me. "What's the big deal, Mom?" he asks grinning. I know alcohol has the power to bring down even this

strong-willed young man, but he doesn't know that yet. I've seen it happen with my dad–the denials, the escalating family arguments, the all-too-early death. I grieve every day for losing this dear man. Is this to be the genetic legacy I pass on to my firstborn son?

It's late. It's so late. Where is he?

I join the chorus of supplicating mothers everywhere, sitting up late into the night with wordless prayers for their children.

— KAY

You're waiting up for me as usual Mom. I've been out on Sand Point having a great time with my friends enjoying the magical northern night sky, laughing long, loud, and hard around a roaring fire. I feel the terrific buzz and warmth of booze. It's way past the time I said I'd be home.

Sitting in your favorite living room chair, wrapped in a bright red robe, it's obvious you have been crying in the dark. We talk. Life, love, my friends, fears, hopes. It is our way of calming each other down in some strange and meaningful way. As usual you ask me not to drink any more, or at least, not as much. To be more careful.
I promise, but not really. Exhausted, we kiss and hug and say "I love you," and go to bed, reassured that everything is okay once again.

— BERNIE

All of a Summer Afternoon

From my front porch
I watched the world lazy by:
kids shrieking home from
the Methodist Sunday school picnic
I had longed to attend;
my cousin running back from
the lake, hair wet and frizzy,
bath towel flung over her shoulder,
boys swinging their bats
bragging about stolen bases,
stolen kisses. What kisses?

I make a tight fist
in my brain as I
hugged my black and white kitten
a little harder,
tucked my twin dolls
beside me on the swing,
ate through to the prizes
in three boxes of Cracker Jacks.

Conformity

One lilac evening

we tossed our hopscotch stones.

Mine went out of bounds

every time

and when your laughter stopped

and I dried my eyes

I said, "Let's play kick the can"

or "Run, sheep, run."

I never can stay

within the lines

when people are watching.

Daring Young Man

On my trapeze

I swing in midair

for hours

never knowing

or caring

about the fall

if it comes

or not

but how I

look to everyone

down there

while I dangle

Reflection   If you wish on the new moon all night

will you get your answer at dawn?

Smothering

You didn't hear

the avalanche crash

and I couldn't tell you

because I was

       smothering.

It was black in the white

and when I tried to move my neck

I felt numb and cold.

My heart told me to pray

or sing or scream

but I knew you

wouldn't hear me

so I huddled inside myself

and waited for spring.

~ MIDDLE YEARS ~

ACCEPTANCE

It began like any ordinary day, the usual mix of what needed to be done today and the leftovers of what should have been done yesterday. I had just put a chocolate cake in the oven. Grandma Sarah's recipe. And then the phone call.

It was Bernie. "Mom, I'm in!" he said. "I have the acceptance letter in my hand."

My heart pounded—the Peace Corps. God knows, we're a service-minded family and to see a son of ours giving away some of his young years, going out of his way for others...what more could we hope for!

I knew George would be so proud. I raced down to the Mill to tell him, but they could not find him. What news I'll have when he comes home. But I had to tell someone. I called my friend Susan. She asked me if I was worried about him going. No, no, no, I told her. And then I realized it: miraculously, pride had overshadowed all my usual worries.

I would never forget this day. Never.

— KAY

Amazing. Far out. Unbelievable. I never thought it would be possible. I am one of President Kennedy's kids. The Peace Corps just accepted me. No idea where I'll be going. Who cares! It will be someplace far away.

Dazed, I read the letter from Sargent Shriver over and over, making sure there wasn't any "not" before the word "accepted." Should I tell anyone? My body is numb with excitement.

I call home. Mom answers, says Dad's working late at the Mill. I tell her the wonderful news. Does her silence stem from elation or anxiety? She congratulates me, and says how proud she is. "Where will you be stationed?" "When will you be leaving?" "How long will you be gone?"

I can tell by the eagerness of her questions that she wants to know more, to find out how I am feeling. I can tell she is excited. She says she can't wait to let family and friends know. Yet, there is hesitancy about what is going to happen next.

At that moment I know my life will never be the same. I am stepping out on my own for the very first time.

— BERNIE

If

If I had stayed
behind the counter
at Woolworth's
and danced at the
West Side Athletic Club
every Saturday night,

if I had continued to picnic
with my family
each Fourth of July
and prayed a novena
with my mother every
Tuesday evening,

then the Swiss Alps
might be just a dream
and the Auld Sod
a strange place where
my grandmother lived.

Our children would be fantasies
and the Rockies another place
on the map
or the words to a
springtime song.

I might read poetry
in many places
but not one line
would be mine
if I had stayed
behind that counter
at Woolworth's
after I sold you
a nickel Hershey bar.

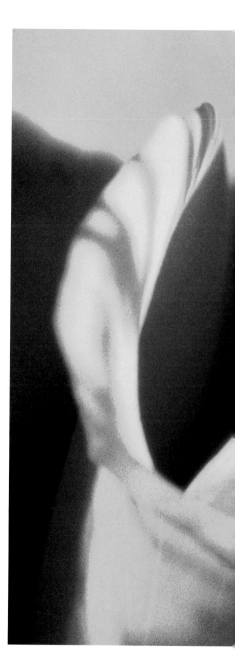

The Journey

Sometimes

it seems

a long way to Bethlehem

The detour I take

is rough and crooked

I struggle to glimpse

a camel or two

no wise men to guide me

If I arrive there

will it be too late

to greet the gentle man

who caresses mother and child

too late to hold Him

We who have sons

know the feeling

Together

When our hearts yelped
unsafe inside our chests
like climbers on a precipice
the life we knew stalled in midair
hung over the edge.

Now we waltz in the kitchen,
relearn forgotten rhythms;
the words sweeten our mouths
like dollops of jam as we sway
to a slower, singular heartbeat.

Reflection She felt wisdom settling in

when she belonged to herself.

At Home

I feel at home in my house.
One day I climbed to the top of the stairs
then fell backward over the edge of darkness;
slivers left scars –
they have healed into rebirth marks
growing pains are more mysterious
than when I was twelve.

I feel at home in my house,
no longer afraid of dark corners
or what's behind closed doors.
I have brushed aside the webs
in narrow stifling closets
answered all echoes in empty rooms.

Fear

To keep the world away
I rattled pans
beat the drum
tied tin cans
on the rear of some
old Chevy.
Fear stalked me
to the cemetery gate
only rusty hinges
scared him away.

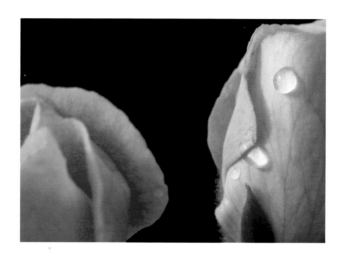

A Tear

It begins

in the hollow of my stomach

where it churns and turns

before it makes its way

toward the dark tunnel

of my throat then

constricts into a knot

tight enough to

push itself up

to the corner of my eye

where it squeezes

from a warm duct

rolls down my cheek

for everyone to see

without knowing

the origin or route or end.

Reflection   Waltz with me into

the deepest heart of wisdom:

forget outer flame.

MOM TO GRANDMA

Where have the years gone? My children have children and even these grandkids are growing into their own: "Turn around and they're two, turn around and they're four..."

I love them all dearly but little things they do or don't do bother me. Todd turned thirteen three weeks ago and still hasn't sent us a thank you note for his birthday present.

What a twisted rope it is that binds us together. I don't really blame Todd for not sending the note. I blame Bernie, his dad. He's the one who should be teaching his young son to be grateful. But it's even more than that. At night in bed, it's not Bernie I blame either. I blame myself for not teaching gratitude to my children, failing them in important ways.

I want so much for all of them — perfect marriages, perfect children, perfect lives — when I know they have a very imperfect mother!

I need to cut them some slack—I wish I could cut myself some too.

— KAY

Mom's not happy. I can sense it as we chat at the kitchen table. I tell her how much fun Todd and Erik had during our Christmas visit. How they enjoyed playing with the gifts from her and Dad. Suddenly she gives me her infamous "look." The force of it startles me. "Is there a problem, Mom?", I ask.

She's not happy with Todd and Erik, because they never send thank you cards for birthday gifts they receive from her and Dad. They will, once in a while, say thank you over the phone or when they see her again, but never a card.

Well, here we go again. Another expectation from Mom of how things should be done.

"I would like you to tell Todd and Erik to write thank you cards to me," she says.

I tell Mom that I'm not willing to be the delivery person for her expectations. She will need to address this directly with her grandsons. She stares at me, and then looks down at the thank you cards she is writing.

— BERNIE

Hope

She walked into my life
wearing a rainbow scarf
bearing a cloudy forecast
hands fluttering like aspen
when the wind grumbles

She begged me to shelter her
from impending fury
and for one foggy moment
I tried to say no.

But then I saw Band Aids
stretched across her copper tan
knew they weren't strong enough
to keep her from bleeding.

The lightning flashed an excuse
to huddle together
until the quiet came
until she felt the calm.

Jigsaw Puzzle

For all the exaggerated

hours after midnight

I tried to fit

the puzzle together:

borders fell easily

flowers, sun, trees.

It was black clouds and jagged rocks

that eluded me

made it impossible

for my groping fingers

to find the missing pieces.

Perhaps today

I shall overturn

the table.

In My House of Words

verbs rest on windowsills

to sprout in April sun:

nouns, proper or not, decorate tables,

want to be polished, picked up,

used in proper places:

prepositions hide behind doors

don't come out unless coaxed;

adverbs and adjectives, more shy,

burrow in closets

behind shoes, old yarn,

boxes of love letters.

But after midnight they all join hands

strut across moonbeams

on the kitchen floor,

sing and dance,

hold tightly to each other

making lovely lonely sounds

in the dark.

Reflection Will we be younger tomorrow

if we pick a bouquet

of Queen Anne's Lace today?

Reflection laughter and pain meld

a celebration in my skin

a catch in my throat

FIRST SHOW

Does every mother wonder as often as I do how so many varied talents can rise out of children raised by the same parents, in the same home, with the same challenges? How is it that one takes to reading encyclopedias, one has a sense of style, one is a natural healer, and another is more comfortable in the woods than in the living room? And now this.

When I first saw Bernie's photos, their shocking beauty caught me off guard. Where did this robust son of mine develop an eye to see into the soul of flowers?

He found this new passion in mid-life almost at the same age that I found the power to

use words. What a mystery this all is. Where do these inspirations come from? There is always a bend in the road and new possibilities waiting if our hearts and hands are open.

I have to make sure he shares the intensity of these photographs with others. I'll invite people over for a show. He'll probably think I'm pushy. That's okay. I may be pushy but I am also proud!

— KAY

It was a command. Not an invitation, a suggestion or a request. It was an outright order. I was to show my photographs of the flowers to her art friends and colleagues. It would be sometime in the fall at her house. No questions asked.

The last time I remember being pushed in such a manner by Mother was when she directed me to go to confession on Friday nights when I was 14 years old.

Once I gathered myself from the shock of the one-way transaction, I realized she was actually honoring me and the art I had created during the summer. She experienced something in the work that triggered a deep aesthetic connection to her artistic passions. I felt like the creative umbilical cord was reattached between us.

I had a fabulous time. Mom had a fabulous time. So did the flowers.

— BERNIE

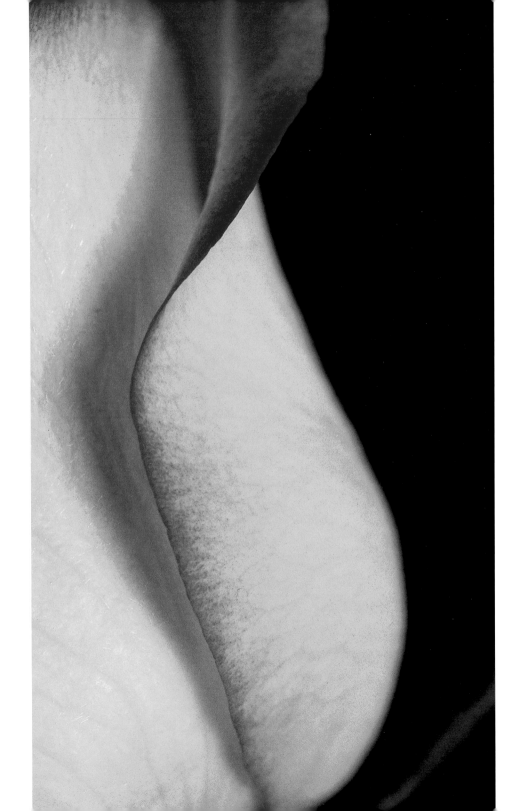

~ OLDER YEARS ~

REVELATIONS

The pack of poems for our book is in the mail to Bernie. I feel like I have sent away a part
of my soul.

I sit with this empty feeling in the half-dark house tonight. Growing old has meant letting go
of so much physical privacy: every part of my body dependent on someone's probing,
diagnosing, medicating. What I've managed to maintain jealously is my emotional integrity, the

memories, both bitter and sweet, and
my spiritual life. Even though I've
encouraged others to write from their
deepest hearts, I've guarded my own
secrets. Or if I've written of them, I've
chosen cautiously to whom I entrusted
them.

I see all that differently these days. I believe
all the intricacies of my life have been
part of God's plan for me. What is most
private to me might be what is most
needed by a person who reads my
words.

Am I giving away too much? No, I
want to mine my life even more deeply,
give it all away. Tomorrow will be a
new day; ah, there is more I need to say.

— KAY

I am swept away by the poems I received today from Mom:
grief, anger, and laughter as I absorb her intimate and
private world. I discover glimpses of her life I never knew
before: childhood adventures under the front porch; the
love and protection of Latin; stories of her in-laws; domestic
abuse; the delightful search for prizes in the bottom of
Cracker Jack boxes; her father slipping Hershey Almond
bars to her as a child.

Some poems speak of things she cannot say any other way.

"My son has gone from childhood to adult.
And though I sometimes strain against the tide,
I must admit that mostly I enjoy
The sight of man emerging from the boy."

Not long ago such exposures of her inner soul were
better kept secret. I am honored that she trusts me enough,
to share.

— BERNIE

Life Drawing

Today I try to color melancholy
but my new box of Crayolas
has too many reds yellows
I slide out the slick points
of black purple
finger their smooth tips
I draw a few swirls and twirls
then stretch a wistful heart
on the rich linen paper
of remembrance.

Reflection

Take my hand,

walk with me to the lake's edge.

We'll skip stones

over the silent surface.

A Pause
on Our 45th Anniversary

Although the tall
summer grasses
on the dune
have turned brown
and the oaks
to crisp, somber rust,
the lake reaches out
before us toward new horizons.

A seagull floats below
the vees of Canada geese
whose flight pattern
heads toward a destination more sure,
more recognizable than ours.

Sentinels

In the March wind
one row of brown, brittle sunflowers
stood, shaking
like defeated soldiers
ordered to stand at attention,
too tired to lift their heads.

Were they forgotten at harvest time
chosen to guard
against the enemy,
a snarling wolf
who lurches across
the fields every spring
on his way to blow the house down?

Bits of Their Lives

She gives up people reluctantly
clutching them
like the warm afghan
she keeps on the sofa.

All sizes, colors, ages
fit comfortably
within her embrace.

She tucks bits of their lives
into her bulging pockets,
takes them out
from time to time
at dusk.

She closes her fingers gently
around each one,
even those lost by distance
or death,
feels their laughter, tears,
their singing.

Lullabies for the Heart

Lullabies

in a small black box

taped to the gurney

close to my ear,

> "When the gentle breezes blow
>
> Violins play their sweet song..."

You insert the tube I can't feel,

guide it deftly to blocked areas.

As my body sinks into the cart

magic melodies flow through arteries.

> "If I could I would
>
> give you wings
>
> to carry you
>
> out of the storm..."

Now you're there.

The balloon inflates, compresses plague.

(More valium, nurse, please)

Two blockages nearly closed

at ninety percent, now open.

> "Tomorrow we'll go to the fair
>
> we'll ride painted horses
>
> with the wind in our hair...."

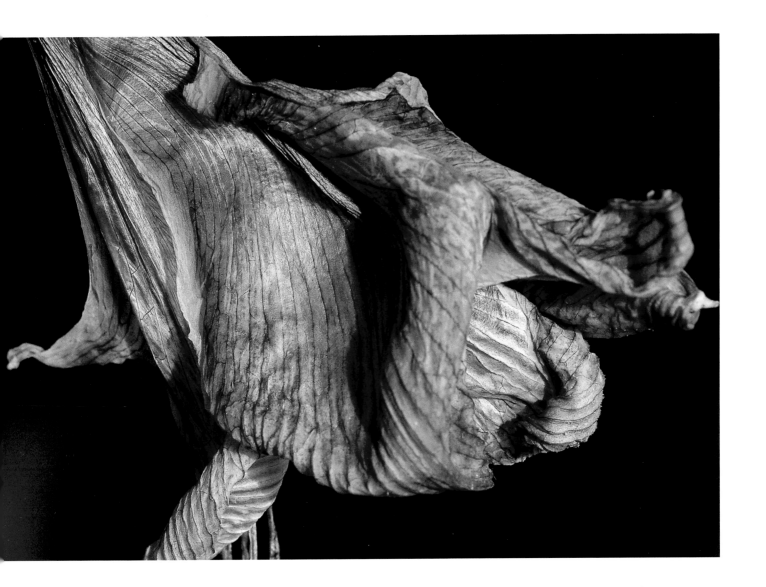

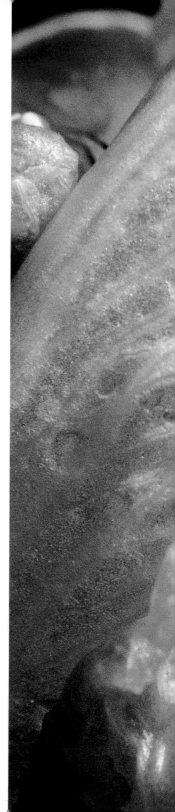

Intensive Care

When her watch said it was time,
time for another five-minute visit,
she again paid homage to him
in his glass house.
She placed one hand
on the cold metal rail
squinted at the monitor
and the maze of tubes,
whispered to the nurse,
traced his zippered chest,
touched his cheek
and breathed because he was breathing

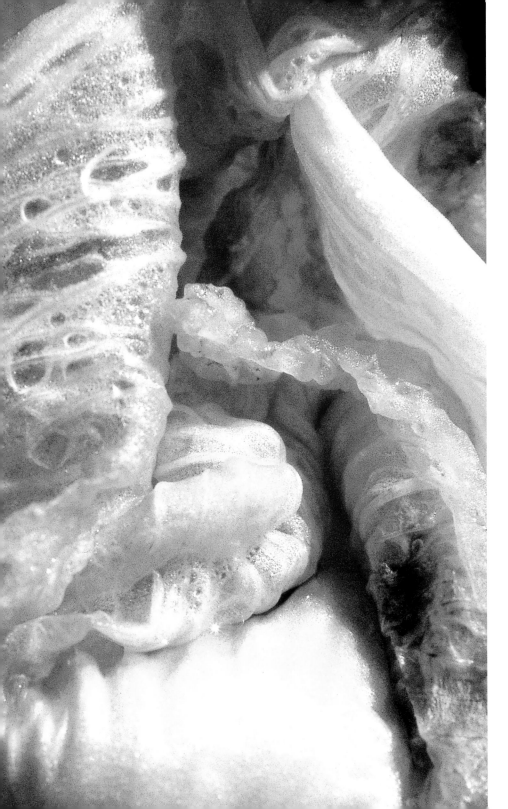

Skeletons

One by one

they shuffle out

when the closet door

squeaks open.

With cold brittle joints

they rattle

into the sunlit parlor

clavicles click

against vertebrae

tibias dangle

from thigh bones.

I try to

dance with them

laugh them away.

They scoff

at my pretensions.

Reflection Never tie a knot you cannot open
with your two fingers.

This New World

"I am a foreigner in the land of old age
And have tried to learn its language."

May Sarton

With ripped map in hand
I wander narrow streets
pass a maze of empty store fronts
search for someone familiar
something safe to lean against.

Folks of every age and color pass,
nod their heads, hurry by.
Strange tongues and garbled words
drift by my ears,
carried on an alien breeze.

Slowly I slide words over my lips,
search for syllables to carry
a reasonable message
one I will understand,
one to be imprinted on my heart.

Reflection The wind whistles low
as milkweed pods spin puffs.
I grow young today.

A REQUEST

Some days I am all body – one wave of ailments after another. And then mysteriously the spirit flows back into me revived by some small delight.

Maybe the wash of afternoon sun on my glass paperweights or I capture the word missing from the poem brewing in my head. Maybe Jack and Betty stop by to say hello or I catch that faint whiff of mint from the kitchen window.

Today Bernie brought an ice cream bar and Killian's beer and that put some starch back into my soul. What a lucky fool I am to find bliss so cheaply!

— KAY

My mother's request surprised me not at all. "Bring me a Killian's Red and a Heath ice cream bar."

Sitting in an uncomfortable hospital lounge chair, wrapped in a white robe, IV tubes in black and blue arms, her eyes shine with a mix of four-year-old delight and twenty-one-year-old anticipation.

The six-pack cools in the fridge at the nurse's station. I remove the paper wrapper and hand her the Heath bar. For a few moments, ice cream dripping down her hand, she sedates her discomfort, and inhales the treat. She licks both sides of the stick.

I wash my mother's tender, frail hands.

— BERNIE

Breed Cemetery

Full moon glow

dazzles tombstones

"Brane – Bradley

Kahn – Kemp"

come all who sleep

under crystalline quilt

        play angel

        play goose

rerun youth

in patterns

around your marker.

A lunatic moon

never lets go

        forget.

About This Birthday

A few days before seventy-five
I check the mirror again
and, sure enough, there are wrinkles
and there is grey in the black hair.
Crepe paper skin barely covers
weak blue veins in arms
that got old before I did.

One drooping eyelid makes me blink
for more artificial tears,
two dropping thighs encased in elephant skin
beg to be covered quickly.
And yesterday when I listed toward the table
I couldn't open the inside cereal wrapper
with my perfectly good fingertips.

But, you know, there's something thirty in there....
The feel of hoisting babies on a smooth
and not so hefty hip,
hugging each one as if love
would, but never could, run out.
Snuggling with them
in a damp tent, then eating
very raw or very burned foil dinners.

And there's something thirty in there...
longing to sway in George's arms
or stomp with him to the Johnson Rag.
And even last night when the couples
jitterbugged and danced the polka
I knew I'd be there again
when the potassium is up
and the ulcer is down.

And there were no wrinkles last night,
but something thirty and wonderful
when George hugged me tight,
kissed me hard, fluffed the pillows,
told me he loved me
for the hundredth time.

Midsummer Dream

When I turned into
a pine stump
I didn't know

chipmunks would cavort
on my chest
wild blueberries
to join them

I didn't know
a choir of ants
would hum mellow music
in the hollow
of my body
sprigs of wild columbine
tickle my face
or the end of my life
be celebrated
in a campfire
where I'd exude light
and fragrance
and from my ashes
another pine

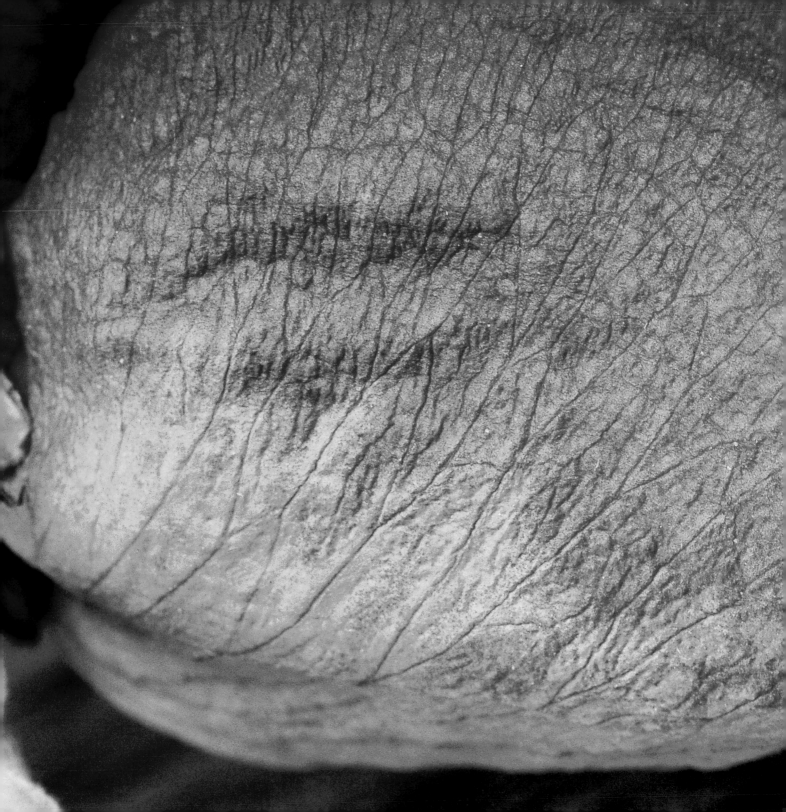

Reflection at age eighty-three

she gave unexpected birth

this time to herself

MOVING ON — BERNIE

We are alone. You lie on your deathbed, covered with a white sheet and blanket, comfortable in a deep morphine sleep. Pooh Bear — a special gift from your great-granddaughter, Andraya — keeps the little girl in you from feeling too afraid and alone.

We are at peace with each other. I feel like a sentry on guard duty. The protector of the Queen Bee. I listen intently to the steady labored drumming as you inhale and exhale. How many heartbeats have you endured in a lifetime of discomfort and pain? The Olympic Gold Medallist for multiple code blues and last rites. The recipient of a weak body that has stuttered and gasped over 85 years. You have pulled off miracle after miracle, repeatedly beating the medical odds with your phenomenal spirit of faith and Irish tenacity.

Sitting here watching you in the semi-dark, I am overcome with the fearful anticipation of this moment since I was six years old. The countless times Dad called saying, "I think this is it," only for you to make another fantastic comeback. Do you know what being on the edge for this long has been like for me? There was always the chance that you could die at any time. Disappear, just like Grandpa. However, the energy around you has been different the past few months. A sense of peaceful acceptance. I have prepared myself all these years for this moment. I am ready to let you go.

Angels of death are gathering. Hovering over us with reverence, they gently prepare to escort you to your next adventure. I will miss you, Mom. The telephone chats. Updates on Todd and Erik. Plans for my next trip. Working on the book. I need to tell you one more time that I love you. *Good-bye, Mom.*

MOVING ON — KAY

Dear Bernie,

Every story you tell about me is true.
But every story you tell about me is
incomplete. There was always more I
wanted to say and do with my life. You
finish the story by adding to it with
yours, will you?

Here beyond time all the differences
that kept us from getting our loving
just right don't matter a tinker's damn.
Here everything is love, pure, simple,
and complete.

This love is my only wish for you....
As ever, Mom

Afterword

The legacy my mother passed on to me I now pass on to you. She taught me that we all speak in a language of the heart and when someone offers us the words, the stories, and images of his or her life, they become humankind's most enduring gifts. It then becomes our turn to pass them on and to offer what we can from our own life experience. Reach out and give away the beauty of everything you have ever known. Reach out and accept the gifts that are offered. Give and give and give again. It is in the giving that we learn to love openly against all odds and to welcome forgiveness and the joy of even the smallest triumphs.

Bernie Saunders

Acknowledgments

Celebration has been a key dynamic in co-creating, nurturing, and bringing alive this project. On behalf of my mother and myself, I want to express my gratitude to the people who supported and guided this book into being.

Bob Blake, Sherry Elmer, Helen Fahrbach, Connie Grabow, Michelle Jahn, Susan Kileen, Laura Kinkead, Betty Schmidt-Kuhr and Jack Kuhr, Bob and Mary Lane, Barbara McAfee, Rusty and Tom McKenzie, Laura Mills, Dr. Robin Price, John Reardon, Richard Schooley, Judy Olausen, Jim Widtfeldt, and Lisa Venable provided insightful gems. Collectively, their support assisted in shaping the book.

The astonishingly talented project team believed in the value and power of this project from the bottom of their hearts. To this amazing group of people I am forever grateful:

Brian Baxter was the passionate, wise guide for how to weave one's way in the book world. His dedication to bringing alive the book was resolute.

Jim Bindas has the ability to take a complex production and publication process and make it an art form. His capacity to be calm and clear during times of creative or emotional conflict was a saving grace.

Anne Hunter's expansive knowledge of the marketing world provided the brilliant focus for how to sensitively connect with the reader.

Ellen Kort knew deep in her soul the core meaning of this book and how important it was to my mother. Love radiates in her fashioning and polishing of words, and in her delicate earth wisdom that I will cherish forever.

Brent Marmo declared in the first fifteen minutes of my initial phone conversation, "I have to do this book." The simple elegance of his book design and attention to detail brought alive the artful relationship of my mother and myself.

Acknowledgments

Patrick O'Brien had tears in his eyes the first time he heard about the idea for the book. He provided invaluable business strategy and compassionate insights for my father and me during the early stages of this project.

Pat Reckrey captured the essence of my mother's soul and heart, and with love and grace genuinely captured her voice in writing. It was an honor working with her in completing the stories my mother and I were unable to finish together.

George Trim was a no-fuss mentor and comrade whose last advice about publishing took place from Cape Cod, in a garden, on his cell phone, sitting in the mud. His energetic spirit will be missed.

Louise Woehrle's enthusiasm and connection with the essence of the book's message created a refreshing on-the-edge perspective, which she enlightened in her descriptive copywriting. She understands the power of story telling.

I thank my siblings, Mary Ann, Dan, Mark, and Sara, and their spouses, for their honest and supportive feedback during the various stages of this project.

My father, George Saunders, provided behind-the-scenes encouragement to my mother when she was alive, and he became my compassionate partner in championing this book after she died. He and I have done many things together, but nothing as precious and meaningful as working together this past year.

Constance Saunders, my wife and artistic soul mate, was with me during my times of doubt about this project. She was always ready, willing, and able to tenderly and firmly guide me back to the path of the original vision. Thank you.

Photographs, stories, and text © Bernard L. Saunders 1997 - 2005

Poems © Kay Saunders 1969 - 2003

Published by Center for Living Art, Inc.
3030 Lakeshore Avenue
Maple Plain, MN 55359
www.centerforlivingart.com

Book and cover design by Brent Marmo, Design:Marmo, Inc.
Cover photo by Bernie Saunders
Author photo of Kay Saunders by Bernie Saunders
Author photo of Bernie Saunders by Margie O'Loughlin
All images were photographed in natural light
Production management by Jim Bindas – Book Productions, LLC

ISBN 13 – 978-0-9768407-0-1
ISBN 10 – 0-9768407-0-7

Printed and bound in Singapore

First printing 2005
10 9 8 7 6 5 4 3 2